21 LIFE SKILLs AFFIRMATIONS FOR POWERFUL LIVING

Heidi J. McFarlane

21 Life Skills Affirmations

21 Life Skills Affirmations For Powerful Living

Copyright © 2013 Heidi J McFarlane

All rights reserved. No part of this book may be reproduced, distributed, or transmitted in any form or by any means electronic or mechanical, including, photocopying, or any information storage and retrieval system, without written permission from the author. For permission requests, please contact the author directly at hmcfar1022@gmail.com

The author shall in no event be held liable for the use, or misuse of the material contained in this publication. The information provided should be used as you see fit and at your own discretion.

Rev. date: 11/2013

ISBN:061575662X
ISBN-13:978-0615756622

Printed in the USA by Amazon Books (www.Amazon.com)
Available in Ebook Format: Kindle

DEDICATION

This book is dedicated to my aunt, Ms. Ambrozene Green (Ms. T). This book is also dedicated to my parents, siblings, family & friends who have supported me, and to those who continue to push forward. I would like to give honor and glory to GOD for giving me his vision and wisdom to give you these words in Love.

*Go to **Now**, ye that say, Today or Tomorrow we will go…*
You know not what Tomorrow brings.
For what is your Life?
It is even a Vapour, that appears for a little time,
then Vanishes away (James 4: 13-14).

21 Life Skills Affirmations

A Gift
*For:*_____

*From:*_____

21 Life Skills Affirmations

CONTENTS

Introduction	i
1. Be Me	7
2. New Beginning	15
3. I Have a Right	21
4. I Believe	28
5. Fear Not	34
6. Go Forward	41
7. Anxious For Nothing	47
8. Made For Me	52
9. I Can	58
10. My Reward	65
11. Gratitude	70
12. Where I Want To Be	75
13. My Voice	80
14. I Am Living	86
15. I Am Loved	91
16. My Comforter	96
17. My Mind	101
18. My Peace	107
19. My Victory	114

CONTENTS

20. I Have The Power	119
21. I Am Fulfilled	125
Epilogue	132
Affirm Yourself and Your Organization	134
Book Recommendations	136
Additional Resources	137

Introduction

Life is full of challenges. I hope that you will read these affirmations to move forward and fulfill your purpose in life. We all have basic needs for food, clothing and shelter, but we also want to be loved, accepted, respected and to be self-actualized; that is to fulfill our life purpose and be all that we can be. We also want to fulfill the expectations we have set for ourselves. The positive words you say to yourself, whispered or audible, coming from your mouth, is an affirmation. Words have power. Words affect your mind, body and spirit. When it comes to motivating oneself, you must constantly read, speak and listen to positive words as they help to determine the action steps that will greatly contribute to your success in life. Whenever you feel like saying a negative word, make every attempt to turn it around by saying something positive.

Read these affirmations as a source of encouragement because you care about your well-being and you care about others around you. Consider affirmations as part of your daily thoughts and commitment to unravel the power, and greatness that is within you. Read these affirmations to help you in transforming into your ultimate self. These affirmations will give you some life tools to remove self-defeating fears, thoughts and behaviors that have been holding you back.

Read these affirmations whenever you are feeling down and negative thoughts attempt to overwhelm your mind. Read these affirmations to remove any mental and emotional block that try to work against you. The words presented in this book will guide you to boldly face your fears, resolve your challenges, and become victorious despite the presence of any obstacles that will arise from time to time.

I am confident that after reading these affirmations, your heart will be enriched, and you will now know how you can positively assert yourself to achieve your highest potential. Many people read and listen to words of encouragement and inspiration, but at times those words do not seem to last, since they are soon forgotten. These affirmations were written for you, because of your desire to make changes in your life for the better, but may not be sure where to begin.

These affirmations will be a guide that will assist you in making your vision and dreams a reality. Whatever you aspire to do, but may not believe that you can achieve because of personal challenges, this book serves as the blue print from which you can learn and implement strategies for a winning mindset. Affirm yourself. Believe in yourself. Stand boldly as you hold your head high knowing that greater is He that is in you, than He that is in the world. Sticks and stones may break the bones, but words can also do damage. Remember, you have the ability to get positive results from the positive and powerful words you speak into your life!

This book was written to help you to use your positive self-talk to go out and claim what is yours and receive all the benefits that are waiting for you. These affirmations were written to give you the strength to carry on. Work these affirmations and let these affirmations work for you. Do not simply read these words without allowing them to make a change in your life. A successful life requires positive self-talk, knowledge, skills, time, effort, commitment, perseverance and the determination to reap a bountiful harvest, coming from seeds you have sewn for a successful lifestyle. You will recover all!

I recently completed a health assessment questionnaire, and based on this report, it stated that positive thinking reduces stress, it leads to better health and higher life satisfaction. Using positive affirmations is a great way to reprogram your subconscious mind from negative thinking to positive thought patterns. They say that most of what you say and do is based on your subconscious thinking. In order to create the life you want, you have to change the way that you think. So by planting statements that reflect the reality of what you want, you are programming your subconscious mind to believe that positive affirmations will help manifest, what you want to see, and realistically experience into being.

Use affirmations as a guide throughout life, they will help to sustain you in your life's journey. Use these affirmations by reading them over and over as part of your daily inner conversation. At the end of reading the recommended ideas on affirmations, you have the opportunity, to get started and write down your own words and ideas that come to mind. You can then create your own affirmations for living your most powerful and most prevailing life yet.

Read your own affirmations in the morning, they will help to direct your path. Read them again to get through the day. Read them in the evening and at night to put your mind to rest. Positive affirmations should become routine in your life. Positive affirmations will help you to keep your focus. Repetition reinforces affirmations and a life of lasting behavioral changes.

Some people listen to affirmations on tapes, but it is best when you write, read, and listen to your own voice. Make affirmations an acquired behavior that occurs automatically. Let it be a habit. Let affirmations instill peace, joy, happiness, and love in your heart. Let affirmations be words of comfort. Let them be words of praise, truth, hope and divine inspiration.

Read this book often. This book is a reminder that we will all fall short and we will all face obstacles, but we have to follow our heart, we have to constantly affirm ourselves and be grateful, no matter the circumstances. To thy own self be true and be positive.

If you would like to make some changes and you need help on developing positive self talk, and work on your own personal affirmations, you can email me, I look forward to hearing from you soon. We all need someone to push us to reach our highest potential. As the popular folk song says, "no man is an island, no man stands alone."

Email: hmcfar1022@gmail.com

Share your own positive affirmations.

The Book Of Affirmations That Will Positively Change Your Life

AFFIRMATION #1

Be Me

I was made for a purpose

There is no other person like me

I am one of a kind, I am unique, and I am worthy

I have an idea and thought that only comes from me

I have a voice, a smile, a walk, and a talk like no other

There is no other human being on this universe just like me

I have a DNA, a thumbprint, and a body make-up,

like no other

I am a wonderful creation

I am me

I Am Being Myself

Who do people say that you are? I AM _____.

Why were you born? If anyone got to choose where, why, and with what DNA they were born with, please let me know. Even with scientific intervention, no one knows the exact nature of their conception. No one choose to be born a certain color, gender or race or in a certain country or century, or by certain parents. You were specifically created and you were born for a purpose, for such a time as this.

At your birth, as a baby, you were the most precious thing in the world to your parents. You beat the odds and you were born. There are so many things that could have happened for you not to be born. Not every baby survives birth! The mother whose child that was never born knows that painful reality.

"All that I am, or hope to be, I owe to my angel mother."

ABRAHAM LINCOLN

Everyday presents an opportunity of growth, to make a difference in your life, and the life of others. When you celebrate your birthday, you celebrate one more year that you get to enjoy living. You are remembering the day of your birth and the opportunity to grow and do more with your life.

I AM ME

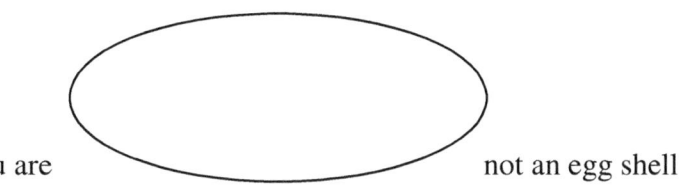

You are not an egg shell! Look inside of yourself; you are not an empty space. You are more than your genetic makeup or your physical body. You have a mind, body and spirit. You have a mind that can imagine and think of great ideas. You have a body that can take you places far beyond your wildest dreams. You have a spirit that is supernatural and stretches far beyond what is visibly seen.

Take an active personal appraisal look at some of the key characteristics that define you. Teach yourself to see the value in you! Get rid of those negative thoughts that often want to pull you down and tell you that you are nothing. Do you like you? You have to like you, since you are a unique individual; there is no one else in this universe or on the planet earth that was made *just* like you. Even if you are an identical twin, you may look alike and share the same DNA or genetic code. But as twins develop, they start to differentiate in their individual personalities due to different environmental experiences and exposure.

Questions

Ask yourself: What do I see when I look at myself in a mirror? Am I being authentic? Am I being true to myself?

Where do I stand with others? How do others see me? What do they say about me? What are my abilities or inabilities? What are my likes or dislikes? What do I value? What are my strengths? What is my calling? What is my passion? What purpose do I serve? What is my destiny? What is my legacy? Do I inspire others when I write, draw, sing, dance or speak? How can I be a better me? What does a better me look like and sound like? How does a better me make me feel, make others feel?

"I have no special talent. I am only passionately curious."

ALBERT EINSTEIN

Use affirmations to stretch yourself and to probe deep down to discover who you honestly are. Begin to focus on what your true purpose in life is; the purpose that enriches your mind, body and spirit. You may not have much silver and gold, but such as you have, you can love yourself. Loving yourself is a valuable gift you give to yourself. In loving yourself, you begin to value you and you can then take steps to become the person you truly want to be. In loving yourself, you are able to see the good in you and in others. You are the only one who can truly lift yourself up. Give yourself the strength needed to stand up when you are weak, when you lack the insight to recognize and feel the power that is inside of you. Appreciate every flaw that you have, because regardless of your imperfections, you are a great design. Remind yourself that you are a wonderful creation. You were beautifully made by a perfect source.

You are AWESOME.

"I am determined to be cheerful and happy in whatever situation I may find myself. For I have learned that the greater part of our misery or unhappiness is determined not by our circumstance but by our disposition."

MARTHA WASHINGTON

With pen and paper in hand, make time to create a list about you. Write down as many great things about yourself that comes to mind as you possibly can. On a daily basis you should review these things while you are preparing yourself in the morning. Review your list; take mental note of your strengths. Look at those things that make you feel special. Read your list aloud as you record the great things about you, and then listen to them. When you listen to great things about yourself in your own voice, it encourages and stimulates your internal being to excel. As your inner being begins to change in alignment with your strengths, your mentality and the way you look at yourself will also start to change. You will begin to experience the true essence of the more confident and powerful you.

You do not have to wait until a great moment of need to utilize the amazing mental and physical strength that you were born with. Do not wait to maximize the great skills, talents and gifts with which you were born to utilize. But how do you know what these are? Since the inception of your birth until present, you might not acknowledge it or have even been aware, but you have been tapping into your great skills, talents and gifts all along. You have certain preferences. You have certain desires. You have certain ideas and thoughts that are unique, and could only come from you, you have ideas and thoughts that only you know.

> *"I am not bound to win, but I am bound to be true. I am not bound to succeed, but I am bound to live by the light that I have."*
>
> ABRAHAM LINCOLN

Who knows more of what defines you than you do? No man knows what is in your heart and soul. You have a vision, a dream and a creative imagination of things that only you can bring forth. You have certain peculiarities about you that make you special. There is something about you that is unlike any other. Never underestimate how great you are, even when others tell you that you are nothing, even when others chastise you and try to do evil against you! Never! Not even once ever think that you are not great!

Start with building up your self-esteem, then work on building someone else's esteem by encouraging others and saying a positive word or two or three. You truly see who you are and what your purpose is all about when you help others, then it will make sense. It is not about the riches that you can get for yourself, but it is about the richness that you bring to someone else.

Focus on those things that make you a better person. Everyday there is an opportunity to change. Some people get a second chance at life when something bad happens, and then they realize that they need to change and start living life to the *fullest.* But do not wait; you may not get that second chance. Let others see what you have to offer. You may amaze yourself in the process. No time than the present to live your best *me.*

Start now and write your own **Be Me** affirmation:

>*>*>*>*>*>*>*>*>*>

AFFIRMATION # 2

New Beginning

Now is my time to create a new day and create a new life

I say, my life has value and my life has meaning

I am here for a reason, now is my season

Now is the time to make my move; it is

time to make my change

My day has come, let this be my first day to reign

Let this be the first hour, the first minute, the first second

I will separate myself from that which is already gone

I will create a brand new me

I am ready for my change and my change is now

I will think it, speak it, hear it, see it and let it be so

This is my rebirth, this is my new beginning

I Am Creating a Brand New Me

There is hardly a better feeling of excitement than owning a new car, a new house, or new clothes. We all like new things. There is something exciting about a new idea, a new relationship, meeting new people, a new job, going somewhere new, doing something new. According to Webster's dictionary, the word *new* means having recently come into existence and to be recently made. No matter what has happened yesterday, each day that you get to see is a new day of discovery, a new day to come into your existence, a new day in your journey of life to start afresh!

Each day is a new opportunity to cease from doing things you have done before which have not yielded the results to fulfill your goals. Today is the inception of something progressive, something positive, for something new and different to happen in your life. Whatever you are accustomed to, each day brings an opportunity for effective change to try to be better, and do something new as you grow and become the very best you.

The process of beginning involves the start of something or a place where something springs forth. There is always a beginning to everything. Everyday there is a chance of a fresh new opportunity and a new beginning of life. When you wake up in the morning, there is something refreshing in the air. You mind, body and spirit come alive again and have been renewed.

> *"The more you praise and celebrate your life,*
> *the more there is in life to celebrate."*
> OPRAH WINFREY

> *"God gave us the gift of life; it is up to us to give*
> *ourselves the gift of living well."*
> VOLTAIRE

Questions:

When are you going to start living your life in abundance? When are you going to start exercising? When are you going to start losing weight? When are you going to start eating right? When are you going to seek out and have that exciting job that you always wanted? When are you going to start enjoying wonderful relationships? When are you going to start giving back and helping others? When are you going to start going on unforgettable vacations? When are you going to start loving yourself?

> *"Every new beginning comes from some other*
> *beginning's end."*
> SENECA

There is no greater time than now to step into the unfamiliar. Stop what you use to do, if it is not working. Do it no more; put it to an end. Begin to utilize your unique creativity. Now is the time to look at your hidden talents. If there is a void in your life, if you feel like there is so much darkness, if you feel like you have not made it or that you have not yet been formed, then let the Spirit deep inside of you move. You have the *power* to push yourself; you are your number one supporter. There is so much more that you can do. There are many others less fortunate who do not have the finances or the resources but have tried and have succeeded. Listen to that inner voice deep inside that is crying out. Have hope and faith, tell yourself that you are finally going to make a change. Stand up, stand out, no more lying down and taking it easy. Use this affirmation to create a new beginning.

> *"Man's main task in life is to give birth to himself, to become what he potentially is. The most important product of his effort is his own personality."*
> ERICH FROMM

Use your new beginning affirmation to reinvent yourself and begin to think new. Write down things that you can do differently that will impact your life. Create a *today checklist*; write down things you need to start doing today. Do not worry about the future, focus on the here and now. Take baby steps and then you can grow. If you want to write that book that you have been thinking of, start now and write down a few words that come to mind. Then come back the next day and write down a few more words. As you start, the words will start to flow and your book will start coming together. PS, don't forget to send me a copy!

What does a new beginning mean to you? Have you started over before? What does a new beginning look like? Feel like? What do you need to do to have a new beginning?

A new beginning can be scary. It can be very anxious. You may feel out of place. You may sweat. You may get aches and pains, but once you push through the negative feelings and emotions, it will be worth it after all. Everything that you are going through someone else has already gone through something similar. Declare your new beginning. Say, let there be and there will be! Once you call it into being and make it happen, you will see good things come out of your new beginning.

Start now and write your own **New Beginning** affirmation:

>*>*>*>*>*>*>*>*>*>*>

_____

_____
_____
_____
_____
_____
_____
_____
_____
_____
_____
_____
_____
_____
_____
_____
_____

AFFIRMATION # 3

I Have A Right

I have a right to produce abundance

I have a right to enjoy life

I have a right to greatness of every kind

I have a right for just a moment in time

I have a right to be fulfilled

I have a right to be successful

I have a right to be filled with increase

I have a right to growth

I have a right to peace and love

I have a right to take control of my destiny

I have a right to perform to the best of my ability

I have a right

I Am Living the Right Life

Having a right means to be in alignment with truth, justice, goodness, equality, freedom, fact and reason. The right time means it is the most opportune, desirable and convenient time. When you have the right of way, you feel privileged and favored. When you are on the right side of town, there is a feeling of been geographically located and of being safe. When you are in your right frame of mind, you think clearly and with more peace to direct your behavior. When you are feeling all right, your heart experiences joyful pulsations, you are happy. One should approach life's experiences with a right and superior mindset that is resolution oriented, and with a certain calm that defies all logic, regardless of the circumstances.

Having a right life means having a balance within your life; a balance in your relationships, your health, your work, your finances, and a balance in your spirit. When you are with the right person or among the right people the world is a happy place, you feel free. When you are thinking, use your subconscious mind to direct your path and make the right things happen. Command your right to accomplish all great things that you set your mind to do. Use I have a right affirmation to value yourself, to focus on and accomplish your life's purpose and goals of success.

With freedom of expression, you have the right to speak your mind. No one is right all the time, but you have the right to be heard. Even though you may feel like a roach in the corner, you have a right to be valued and be effective. Unlike the animals, we have a powerful instrument called the tongue that we can utilize to change the atmosphere and make things happen. With rights you are given access and allowed to go places that are restricted. You can go from a poverty stricken shanty hut to the Queen's palace.

> *"Freedom consists not in doing what we like, but in having the right to do what we ought."*
> **POPE JOHN PAUL II**

Like the early pilgrims and the founding fathers of the American Constitution, many people have risk their lives to stand up for what is right so that many others may live a better life. Are you standing up for your rights so that you and others can live a better life? The *US Bill Of Rights* gives one free exercise of religion, freedom of speech, the right to peaceful assembly, the right to bear arms, the right to protect your property, the right against unreasonable searches and seizures, the right to a speedy and public trial by an *impartial* jury. Along with constitutional rights, one has jurisdictional rights which gives you power and authority over a certain area. Now more than ever, you have to fight for your rights when others who are oppressed by nature attempt to deny you your declared rights. Sometimes people die in defending their rights. But, without rights there is abuse of power and freedom is either limited or restricted.

To fight for your rights stems from the inner call to fulfill basic needs and to prevent them from being taken away. The most common basic needs that we know of includes physiological need, safety and security needs, belonging and love needs, esteem needs, self actualization needs and spiritual needs. Moreover, when we affirm and fulfill our basic needs, we experience positive interpersonal feelings and a state of well-being and contentment; we feel happy.

"All the evidence that we have indicates that it is reasonable to assume in practically every human being, and certainly in almost every newborn baby, that there is an active will toward health, an impulse towards growth or towards actualization."

ABRAHAM MASLOW

We all need to nourish our bodies and in so doing we fulfill our physiological needs, otherwise, we cannot survive. In fulfilling safety needs, there is peace, stability and freedom from treat or harm. With security we are protected and feel less exposed, vulnerable and isolated. The social need for belonging means that we seek the approval and affection of family, friends, groups and organizations to feel apart of something and feel that we belong. Love is the greatest law that if everyone followed, the world would be a better place to live. Love is freedom, it is not a matter for rules or regulations. Love speaks out for justice and protection from harm. Love overcomes all.

The ability to achieve anything in life is directly related to your self-esteem, it makes the difference between your success and failure. Your number one relationship is with self. In fulfilling your self-esteem, you act independently and assume responsibility for your actions, goals and desires in life. In fulfilling self-actualization needs, you should know what actions steps are to be taken. When these actions are engaged to your satisfaction, you'll feel like you have fulfilled your *true* potential.

In a reading of Our Daily Bread, "The Power of Affirmation" it talks about a recent study of 200,000 employees who were interviewed regarding what was the missing ingredient to their productivity. The study found that appreciation and affirmation was at the top of the list of what employees wanted most from their supervisors. This study showed that even in the work place, receiving affirmation is also a basic human need. Even on the job you have the right to have your basic needs be met, you have the right to be all that you can be.

In looking beyond ourselves and what the evolutionary theorists say, we realize that we did not create this universe and we did not design ourselves, but that there is an infinite Creator who made us. Our spiritual needs become met when we see that there is more to life than our fleshly body, and that there is a higher power in control. Focus on your right to have your basic needs be met; to be free and have the freedom to be yourself. When you stay in the right, you avoid the negative. Affirming what is right makes you aligned with your life purpose. Staying in the right is a motivator for relationship with self and with others.

What does having rights mean to you? How does having rights make you feel? What rights do you need? How can you get those rights met?

Living the right life, starts with you. If you talk right, act and react right, others around you become drawn to you. You become a leading force, no matter what your current position.

Start now and write your own **I Have A Right** affirmation:

>*>*>*>*>*>*>*>*>*

_____

_____

_____

_____

_____

_____

_____

_____

_____

_____

_____

_____

_____

_____

_____

AFFIRMATION #4

I Believe

I believe I can do all that I was made to do

I believe that I have control of my life

I believe that what I want will come to me

I believe that if I ask it will be given unto me

I believe that if I seek, I will find

I believe that if I knock, the door will open

I believe that with God, I am the author of my faith

I believe and trust that I am a winner

I believe in my greatness & the greatness of others

I believe that I can overcome all things that come against me

I believe that I will not die, but have life everlasting

I believe in you and I believe in me

I Believe I Can Do All Things

What do you believe? You cannot change your circumstance until you believe that it is possible to change. You have to accept that what you believe is true, genuine or real. You have to visualize and find ways to create that vision that you see through your mind's eye, even when you do not have the absolute proof. Why do we choose to believe the negative more than the positive? Why do we believe more that we will fail than we will succeed? If you only believe then you can see what's ahead of you.

> *"Believe in yourself! Have faith in your abilities! Without a humble but reasonable confidence in your own powers you cannot be successful or happy."*
>
> NORMAN VINCENT PEALE

If you choose to believe the positive, then you can fulfill your purpose with greater ease and enjoyment. Believing has helped a man locked up in an African prison to become the president of his country. Believing has made many athletes win gold medals in the Olympics. Believing has allowed many people to face danger, to step out and risk their lives so that they can help others and make a difference. Believing instills hope and faith. Believing helps you to overcome fear. Believing has allowed the sick to be healed, the blind to see, the paralyzed to walk and even the dead to return to life. Yes, how many people have you heard or seen who were pronounced dead but are now proclaiming life.

We have heard of people who should have died or were in some perilous situation but were able to survived because they believe that they would overcome and live to tell their tale. Therefore, all things, not some things, whatsoever you shall ask in prayer, believing, you shall receive (Matt 21:22, KJV). In believing, you have a firm conviction that something is true. In believing, you utilize your innate skills, you listen to that inner voice and in spite of how things appear, you overcome your fears to do what you have to do to get ahead.

Do you adhere to the principle that seeing is believing? Do you believe everything that you see is true? Is what we see, merely a perception or state of the brain or a functioning of the nervous system? How does the brain interpret what it sees? Is what we see, really what is present? Our belief system, like our perception is based on our previous knowledge of something. For example, if you see a small fish like a piranha and do not know what a piranha is, you might not be fearful of the danger that can occur from being in the presence of this flesh eating fish. Only after seeing the harm of what a piranha does then you will believe that it is a dangerous fish.

According to Cognitive Science, there is a middle realm between what we pre conceive and post perception (what is seen). It is interesting how the forces of nature and the spiritual realm seem to act upon our belief system which further validates or gives forthcoming evidence (preconception) to that which is not yet seen (post perception)[1].

Questions

Does your belief system consist of absolutes such as never, musts, shoulds, and cannots? Is *everything* really awful, terrible or horrible? Can you really not stand it? Where is holding these beliefs getting you? Is it helpful or self-defeating? Where is the evidence to support the existence that *everyone* is awful and *everything* is terrible? There is good and bad everywhere.

Strive for a rational belief system where you can feel disappointed, frustrated, sad, concerned, or annoyed, but you do not get very depressed, anxious, hurtful, full of rage, bitter, jealous and have low frustration tolerance. Do not become that negative person that everyone hates to be around. Strive to become that true loving human being that was created by God.

Use I believe affirmation to build yourself up and establish your faith knowing that regardless of the circumstances, you can see the goodness in yourself and those around you. Even though life may seem difficult, you should know that whatever you are going through is only for a moment and will not last forever. You just have to believe that. Use this affirmation to strive for greatness and let positive thoughts of success flow into your mind. Use this affirmation so that when you believe in yourself

---

[1] [http://ase.tufts.edu/cogstud/papers/seebelie.htm]

and when others do not believe in you, you will receive that which you ask and believe to receive. *You can ask and you will receive,* it's just a matter of timing. Have patience and seek knowledge and understanding to know that things might not happen immediately when we would like it to happen, but that *something* is happening.

> *"You just have to believe in yourself when you've got something, and just keep pounding on the door, because if you pound long enough, somebody is going to open it."*
>
> CYNTHIA WEIL

Have an "I believe" mindset, "I can" mindset, "I will" mindset, and a "just do it" mindset. Whatever the circumstance, do not let fear stop you. Seek to believe and endeavor to look, hear, speak, walk and feel all that is in the world for you to enjoy. What you now see, hear and feel could be the best experience of your life. You have heard it a thousand times, let nothing or no one hold you back, sometimes the only thing stopping you is you.

Start now and write your own **I Believe** affirmation:

>*>*>*>*>*>*>*>*>*>

_____

_____

_____

_____

_____

_____

_____

_____

_____

_____

_____

_____

_____

_____

_____

_____

_____

AFFIRMATION # 5

Fear Not

When trouble rises up against me

When times look dim like there is no help

I will lift up my head

I will cry out & rejoice, I will speak up and be heard

I will not be swayed by negative situations

& things that come against me

I will not be afraid of people that set them selves against me

I will rise up and see all my enemies fall by the way side

I will fight the battle tall & strong

I will rejoice for I have won

Forever, I will not be afraid

I Am Fearing Nothing

Fear is often seen as a displeasing emotion that signals some impeding danger will happen. Fear, however is useful when it pushes you to do great and honorable things. Whenever you are feeling fearful about taking on a venture or new endeavor, just listen to that inner voice telling you to live your life anyway, and do not let fear hold you back from achieving your dreams.

"The only thing we have to fear is fear itself."

FRANKLIN D. ROOSEVELT

Overcome fear with joyfulness knowing that you are have a courageous heart and mind that can help you to endure forever. In conquering your fear you will receive your reward and the glory that you desire. Once you overcome a fear, that fear will never affect you like it did before. In the midst of impeding danger or dread, just relax and believe that things will work out for the good. Believe that you have the courage and the power to overcome fear. In due time you will receive that which you set out to achieve. You have already won and at the right time all that you want will be yours.

Fear prevents many people from pursuing and conquering their dreams. Fear stops, fear cripples, fear blinds, fear makes the unreal seems real. Fear is like punishment. It holds you in bondage. When you are fearful, you do not feel free, you feel confined to a certain state of being. If you have fear, you do not think about others, in fear you grow out of love for yourself and others. Do not let fear destroy your life, stand strong and firm. Do not let others instill fear in you. Fear can be contagious especially when it is among a group of like-minded people. Social fear causes destruction in our world.

Destruction, distress and anguish will come against them that cause fear to come in your life. Do not let your heart be troubled, you might have to wait a while, but keep your head held high and experience your joy because your success will come. In everything that you do there will be "nay-sayers" or pessimists, there is someone who will not support you in your endeavors and say that you cannot do something. Eventually when things start to turn around and you start to succeed, they will be put to shame. They will then want to come around you and applaud you for your courage.

Do not let fear stop you from pursuing your dreams because you know in your heart that you have goals and aspirations that you want to accomplish. Many people give up their dreams because of the fear of failure. They sabotage their dreams, thinking that they are not capable. When circumstances begin to get in your way, stay focused and maintain a mindset of already achieving what you set out to achieve. Call it done!

"What is needed, rather than running away or controlling or suppressing or any other resistance, is understanding fear; that means, watch it, learn about it, come directly into contact with it. We are to learn about fear, not how to escape from it."

JIDDU KRISHNAMURTI

You have a right and the ability to produce success; so do not let fear stop you. Public speaking is one of the biggest fears in the world. Slow your thoughts down, do not be afraid to step on that stage and speak in front of people. Many people fear what others might say about them on stage; how they look, how they sound, what they said, how they acted. With practice, by learning relaxation and public speaking techniques, you can let go and be more at ease. You may get valuable feedback and gain success when you put yourself on a stage and just let your voice be heard. What you say on a platform may help someone else to grow and develop as a speaker.

People fear others they do not know and understand. Sometimes when you are in unfamiliar places and around unfamiliar individuals, you get feelings of social anxiety or shyness. With social anxiety, your heart beats faster, your palms get sweaty, you body starts to react in extreme ways, you start to freeze up and you feel unable to interact. These emotional changes and sensations make you want to avoid the situation. Learn to step outside your comfort zone, put yourself out there, network, speak up, speak to different people, soon you will fulfill your goals of feeling confident and being around others in different social situations.

We also fear death greatly, but all our days are numbered and we all will eventually die. Accept death as a part of the life cycle. Do not waste your time worry about death, instead fill each day with as much joy as possible, enjoying life. Life is short; it is not about here today, gone tomorrow anymore, it is here today, gone today.

Learn techniques to overcome your fears. When you are feeling fearful, sing a happy song, make a joyful noise, think of something funny, think of loving and happy thoughts. There is sweet victory that is very valuable when you know that you have conquered your fears. When you overcome your fears, it brings you peace and understanding. Moreover, if you have a phobia or some extreme fear that is stopping you from succeeding or even functioning well in life, get help fast, do not use your own wisdom, seek professional help. Once you learn how to overcome your fears, you will get the strength and be a testimony to help someone else to overcome his or her own fear.

Use this affirmation to help yourself to gain wisdom and learn ways to overcome your fears. Whatever your fears, condition yourself with daily affirmations on freedom from those fear. Build your self-confidence and release yourself from the emotional bondage of fear. Life change only happens through repetition and courageously taking daily action steps forward. Leap into unfamiliar possibilities. Do not be afraid of failure because of anticipated shame and humiliation.

Affirmation strategies for coping with fear:

- Validate the source of fear, where is the real evidence?
- Use reality affirmations- "My fear is not real"
- Regulate fear by using positive words of affirmation

What are you currently afraid of? Envision yourself overcoming this fear. What does your fear look like? What do you need to do to overcome your fear? What has prevented you from overcoming your fear? How would it make you feel to overcome your fear?

Take small action steps to develop yourself and overcome the fears that are inside of you. Have a plan of action to follow through on what you need to do to release yourself from that which is holding you back.

Start now and write your own **Fear Not** affirmation:

>*>*>*>*>*>*>*>*>*>

AFFIRMATION # 6

Go Forward

Now is the time to move ahead

Not later, not tomorrow

I will overcome obstacles in my way

I will use my creative imagination

I will bring forth an idea that is to come to life

I will proclaim it & make it so

I will be productive & grow in great increase

I will take back all that was lost or stolen from me

I will push ahead & I will go forward

I Am Going Forward

To go forward is a command to proceed to whatever action is required to get you to a point. If you are not going forward you are at a stand still or you are going backwards. We often live our lives based on what has happen in the past. We want to stay in the past and blame somebody. We become at ease with not moving forward. When you refuse to go forward you focus on the negative memories, negative hurt and pains and so you are going backwards and not moving on. Your heart becomes hardened, your neck becomes stiffened, when you walk backwards eventually you will fall, you will get hurt, your bones will break, you will feel pain and you may even die if you do not heal. Stop stepping backwards. How can you see what is behind you when you are backing up? Your eyes are in front of you and not behind you. Stop thinking and living in the past.

> *"Nobody gets to live life backward. Look ahead, that is where your future lies."*
> ANN LANDERS

Have you forgiven someone seventy times seven? When you forgive others for what they have done to you in the past, it helps you most and not the other person. Most people do not even remember that they did something to you in the past. They are not feeling any pain, while you go around life carrying that extra burden. Hurting people hurt and the only way to break the cycle is to start being more loving. Sometimes the same things that we accuse others of doing to us and we do not want to forgive them for, we are also are guilty of doing the same to someone else. No one is perfect, but we should all strive to be good to ourselves and to others.

> *"March on. Do not tarry. To go forward is to move toward perfection. March on, and fear not the thorns, or the sharp stones on life's path."*
> **KHALIL GIBRAN**

Use this affirmation to free your mind and body from the past. Do not throw yourself into a mental prison or infirmary. If you are caught up in issues of the past, release or free yourself today. Get out and enjoy your freedom. There is no time than the present to create new memories and new habits, new rituals of doing things better. Use today to focus on moving forward, forgiving someone and creating new life experiences. Have a ready mind and a willing heart to change your life. Life is ever changing, our bodies are changing. We have to keep up with our health and the best way to have a healthy body is to have a healthy mind free from negative and backward thinking.

Going forward brings you to the place that you want to be. It is good to have a guide and direction on your journey to go forward. You will need instructions and knowledge in the way in which you will go. You need to have an idea of where you are going. Going forward is like pushing your way towards your life's purpose. Be open to saying a kind word to someone who has hurt you. Start moving forward by developing relationships and opportunities. If you want to move forward, do not be afraid to read an inspirational book that can give you ideas, watch an inspirational movie or talk to someone who can get you to where you want to go. Chances are that from talking to others and seeking out resources on what you want, you will get the knowledge you need to help you.

> *"Even if you fall on your face, you're still moving forward."*
> **VICTOR KIAM**

In going forward you will learn patience, wisdom and understanding. You need not be too hasty so as to make foolish decisions. Take the time to push ahead in your thinking and your actions. Do not be afraid to go forward, you have the power and strength to push yourself to instead of going one mile to go two miles, then three miles until you have completed a marathon. Claim your present because it is yours for the taking. You *win* a race when you *start* the race, *run* the race and *push* yourself first over the finish line.

Encouraging steps to moving forward:
- Realize that we are all human and we all make mistakes
- Forgive yourself and learn from your mistakes
- Plan a comeback strategy
- Realize that you can't control anyone else's behavior but your own

- Appreciate that change is possible
- Acknowledge and learn from the past, but remove toxic behaviors and relationships
- Focus on new opportunities and new possibilities

Start now and write your own **Go Forward** affirmation:

>*>*>*>*>*>*>*>*>

AFFIRMATION # 7

Anxious For Nothing

I will not let anxiety take control of my life

I will not be over whelmed by things

I will not worry about tomorrow

I will not let my heart be troubled

I will not be afraid

I will not be pressed done and broken

I will overcome negativity & have the freedom to enjoy life

I will see the goodness in all that I do

I will be grateful for the opportunities that come my way

I will be calm in the midst of my storm

I will enjoy my peace & tranquility

There is nothing hidden that will not be known

There is nothing broken that will not be fixed

I will be anxious over nothing

I Am Anxious For Nothing

Anxiety is an emotion that signals a downcast uneasiness of the mind and body regarding an anticipated event that may or may not happen. This uneasy and disturbing feeling signals that there is some impending danger or threat about to happen. Anxiety can weigh you down. Anxiety is a emotion that is common to everyone's life journey. Spending sleepless nights worrying about your life, bills, finances, what you will eat, and what you will wear the next day is not really beneficial. Anxiety can make you more anxious during your day because of the stored up thoughts constantly going through your mind.

Anxiety causes poor concentration at work, at school and at play, it is a distraction. Anxiety deprives you of the adequate sleep that you need, it causes mental distress. Anxiety causes harmful lifestyle habits such as overeating, cigarette smoking, or using alcohol and drugs. Anxiety causes heart problems, breathing problems and overall sickness in your mind and body. Anxiety over a period of time can have very bad effects on your health and well-being. Chronic anxiety can sap you body's resources from responding appropriately therefore self healing and self preservation mechanisms become defective.

Take time to take action and take care of upcoming tasks to avoid feeling anxious about it. De-clutter your environment so that you can think clearly. Having a better understanding of what ails you can sometime help you to overcome your anxiety.

Think of all the alternatives. Conjure up images that focus on positive outcomes. Be open to different ways of looking at things instead of one narrow way. If you are anxious over something wrong that you did, you need to seek action, if it is forgiveness, you need to make amends to set *your* mind at ease.

In the moments of anxiety, be grateful for what you do have, knowing that things can be a lot worst. Overcome anxiety with gratitude and kind words of hope and encouragement. Listening to relaxing music can help calm you mind before an upcoming test or trial. Inhale relaxing scents that can reduce tension in the body and help increase mental clarity. Learn breathing techniques that can help you to relax. Exercising can create chemicals in your brain to reduce your anxiety. When you conquer anxiety you will receive peace in your mind, body and spirit.

> *"Comedy is defiance. It's a snort of contempt in the face of fear and anxiety. And it's the laughter that allows hope to creep back on the inhale".*
> WILL DURST

Focus on the big picture or ultimate goal of your purpose. In the midst of taking risks, have patience, relax and believe that things will work out for the good. Believe that you have the strength and the power to overcome your anxiety. In some of your most anxious moments, you can be strong. Through anxiety, give yourself the courage to do things that you would not otherwise think of doing but will feel great after doing it.

> *"Anxiety is part of creativity, the need to get something out, the need to be rid of something or to get in touch with something within."*
> DAVID DUCHOVNY

Use this affirmation to help you gain the confidence to overcome your anxiety. Do not let anxiety turn into a panic attack where it affects your life to the point where you cannot function. If you have anxiety that seems too hard to control, get the help you need to overcome it. Learn to refocus your thoughts on what is present and on what you can do right now to change the situation. When you worry about tomorrow you are wasting time from enjoying your today. My mother always says do not let anyone steal your joy. Anxiety is like a thief that steals your time from enjoying the *present*. Likewise, do not let anything or anyone take away from your opportunity of enjoying today.

What does a life free from anxiety looks like? Remember a time when you experience peace, relaxation and comfort, where were you at, who were you with, what were you doing? Write your freedom from anxiety affirmation. Visualize what that freedom looks like. How do you want to feel? What do you need to make it happen?

Start now and write your own **Anxious For Nothing** affirmation:

>*>*>*>*>*>*>*>*>*>

AFFIRMATION #8

Made For Me

Light and darkness were made for me

The evening and the morning were made for me

Day and night were made for me

Water in the ocean and stars in the sky were made for me

The air above is not man made, it was made for me

The birds that fly and every living animal were made for me

The grass and the fruit trees were made for me

Everything that I want in Life is made for me

Whatever my goal, vision, dream, has been made for me

I just have to claim it and take control because

it was already made for me

This World Was Made For Me

The earth is a wonderful place that is made for us to enjoy. The birds that sing, the twinkling stars, how great is this place that we call home. We are amazed by the great Wonders of the World. We can now travel thousands of miles into space to the moon and back. From traveling into space, man has gotten to see astounding and magnificent depictions of the universe.

From the beginning of time everything has been created for our livelihood. We as human beings are able to stay alive by eating the food around us, because without it we would not survive. They say food is the staff of life. The air we breathe is also created for our survival. We can go a while without eating but we can only live for a few minutes without air. We take for granted the air around us until we have to be dependent on a breathing machine such as an oxygen concentrator or a ventilator. Learn to take deep breaths and do deep breathing exercises on a daily basis.

When you exhale and breathe out, you release pollutants from your body. When you inhale negativity, you will exhale negativity. Your body and mind works harder when you are in a polluted environment and in negative surroundings. Your blood pressure and heart rate is higher during negative situations. Just breathing fresh air, having a fresh mind set, and being around positive people will give you more energy, make you feel sharper, and increase your overall sense of happiness and well-being.

Water is a vital source of life. The average adult body is made of 60-75% water. The water that you drink helps you to replace the fluids that you lose on a daily basis. As a human being, you have to constantly hydrate your mind and your body. Most sources state that the brain is 78% water. Water gives you energy to withstand those dry days when you have to put out physical and emotional fires. As a detoxifier, water helps to flush your system of toxic emotions that causes headache, stress, depression, confusion, chronic fatigue, and pain. Water is so useful; it helps protect you from the negative elements around you. They say milk does a body good, but water does a body better.

Without light, we would be in utter darkness. We have seen shows that depict what it would be like if we did not have light. People would be fighting against each other; there would be constant turmoil. In certain parts of the world where an abundance of sunlight is not available, people suffer from depression and sadness. Lack of sunlight also causes vitamin D deficiency diseases. Vitamin D is the only essential vitamin that our bodies manufacture through sun exposure. Vitamin D is a power source that is needed for cell communication through out the body, it helps the immune system, helps with your weight, lowers risk of heart attack, and helps keep the brain working into later years.

We need all the natural resources that we can get. Many individuals like to live in geographic areas that have a lot of sunshine. They want to move to the tropics. The different seasons are great, but there is something about sunlight that is needed to lift your mind, body and spirit. Without sunlight as a source of energy, many plants and humans do not survive; they just wither away and die.

The separation of day and night, gives us a balance between being awake and being at rest. This allows our body to grow and be more productive. The foundation of the earth has being created, everything that your heart desires has already been made for you. The fish in the sea, the birds in the air, the animals on land have been made for you. There is a balance to the food you eat including the fruits, vegetables, meats and grains that have been made for you.

There are people right now; who do not know where their next meal is coming from, who are taking their last breath, who do not have clean water to drink, who are imprisoned and do not get to see much sunlight, and who do not feel at peace. Eat a balance diet, take deep breaths, enjoy fresh air, drink plenty of fresh water, soak up the sunlight, get enough rest, and be thankful for what has been made for you.

"Just as treasures are uncovered from the earth, so virtue appears from good deeds, and wisdom appears from a pure and peaceful mind. To walk safely through the maze of human life,

one needs the light of wisdom and the guidance of virtue."

BUDDHA

Once you can create an idea in your imagination, the supplies are already available for you to put your creation together. Since someone else may have already accomplished an idea you already thought of doing, provisions are readily available for you to create or enhance your own concepts. Use the tools around you that have already been created to make your own dreams come through. Work through the people around you to help bring your vision into reality.

Use your hands to further shine and let the light that has been created within you shine. Do not wait, go get what has already been made for you. You were made to have dominion over *all* the earth, every living thing was made for you. You were made to create good things in this earth and not to deplete what you have. You were made to have control and to not hold back on all the gifts and talents that have been given to you.

What dreams or vision of success do you currently have? What does your dream or vision look like? Where are you? Who are you with? What are you doing? Write down your made for you affirmation. How does accomplishing your dreams make you feel? Write done what you need to do to make it happen. What skills or resources do you currently have to make your dreams come through?

Start now and write your own **Made For Me** affirmation:

>*>*>*>*>*>*>*>*>*>

_____

_____

_____

_____

_____

_____

_____

_____

_____

_____

_____

_____

_____

_____

AFFIRMATION #9

I Can

I can start all over

I can rebuild myself

I can release the negative past &

look at a positive future

I can embrace change

I can ask for what I want

I can face tomorrow

I can welcome success

I can increase my current condition

I can direct my own path

I can have all that I put my hands to

I can control my destiny

I Can Do All Things

I can? Yes, you are able. You are capable. You can be, do and want so many things. You can know, understand, influence, love, dream, hope, think, imagine, follow, jump, laugh, cry, run, read, write, sing, dance, walk, talk, see, hear, and feel. You can be good, you can be bad. You have the ability do all things that you put your mind to. Hold fast to that belief and you will see the results that you seek. The word can is an active word, which means that something is activated. Can is the confirmation of something. The possibilities are endless if you can. There is nothing too hard for you to do. The options are there when you focus on what you can do. Give yourself permission to do the things that you believe that you can do.

Do you conform and are swayed by others or things that seem impossible? It is by testing that you will know your capabilities. How does a lion know that it is strong and everyone knows it as the king of the jungle? It is by overcoming those other animals in the jungle that a lion knows that it is tough and has the strength to overcome rivals. In life, you will face many jungle situations, but you have to be like a lion and show others that you are strong and that you are an over-comer.

The words "I can" stimulates motivational urges on the inside, this gives you energy to take action. You live in lack when you say that you can't. You have given up and feel defeated when you operate in cannot versus can. The word *can* motivates you to step forward despite challenging issues and circumstances. The popular serenity prayer states:

"God grant me the serenity to accept the things I cannot change, the courage to change the things that I can, and the wisdom to know the difference."

REINHOLD NIEBUHR

Who is the perfect person? There is no perfect person. Life is not perfect. There are individuals who have no feet, but are running marathons with prosthetics to support charities or a worthy cause. Moreover, there are those who have feet but refuse to exercise and walk around a block. There are those who are blind, but have thriving careers or independently operating successful businesses. There are those who are deaf and dumb but are political activist, artists and great contributors of this generation.

I am totally amazed by Joni Eareckson, a quadriplegic (paralyzed from the neck down) activist who has had her own radio show for over 30 years. Wow, we might think how does someone who is quadriplegic overcome the odds to become a radio personality. When I first heard Eareckson on the radio, I had to listen intently as I was in disbelief that she had not much use of her limbs but yet had her own radio show for such a long time. During one show, she talked about wanting to be a paraplegic (paralyzed from the waist down), but she stated that even with being a paraplegic, she would not be totally content with her life. Eareckson says "don't look at your limits, think about the possibilities... have hope; God can do a lot, a lot more than you realize, in an impossible situation"[2]

From reading Eareckson's story, the road to where she is currently at was not easy. She had to make the important decision not to give up, but to gain new skills and a fresh determination to help herself and help others around the world. She has written over 50 books and has received many awards and honors for her courage to do all that she can do.

If you are looking for a job and you are thinking that because you do not have steady work experience and you do not have a certain degree, that you will not and a cannot get a job. Regardless of what you lack on paper, be reminded and be encourage that you have good qualities that any employer will find valuable. Utilize what you can do to go out and get that job that you desire.

Be encouraged to make little changes that can be made. Sometimes the little changes can mean a lot later on. Use wisdom to make changes that make a contribution and make a difference. Be content with what happens as long as you have done your best, so that you can learn from every situation that which is good, acceptable and perfect.

---

[2] http://www.joniandfriends.org/radio/5-minute/limited-resources/

"Man's unique reward, however, is that while animals survive by adjusting themselves to their background, man survive by adjusting his background to himself."

AYN RAND

Imagine you are climbing up a mountain and you are almost there, but then you realize that the terrain has gotten harder to navigate, you then start to feel out of breath and tired. Saying the word I can, gives you that extra momentum to keep going to the top, where you can then enjoy the view, and see above the rest of the landscape. Exhale and know that you did it.

Use "I can" affirmation to overcome those obstacles and mountains in your life. "I can" taps into that inner potential and reservoir that you have deep down inside. We have heard stories of people who have lifted cars and trucks off their loved ones in life or dead situations. Many of these people never would have thought that they had the strength and courage to do the things they did. When you operate in the spirit of "I can", great things will happen. Think and speak "I can" and be open to the endless possibilities. We have a strength inside us that is full of greatness. We can do so much if we allow ourselves to become in touch with that inner reservoir.

"Today I choose life. Every morning when I wake up I can choose joy, happiness, negativity, pain... To feel freedom that comes from being able to continue to make mistakes and choices – today I choose to feel life, not to deny my humanity but embrace it."

KEVYN AUCOIN

Remember a time when you experienced an "I can" moment. Who were you with? What were you doing? Use this affirmation to make things happen in your life. Yes, you can!!!

Start now and write your own I Can affirmation:

>*>*>*>*>*>*>*>*>*>

Affirmation # 10

My Reward

I will not be condemned for rejection is natural

I will not take offense to those who reject me

For they will be judged accordingly

because they do not accept me

If any one will not welcome me

I will search for worthiness within & there will I dwell

I have not lost because of man's rejection

Wisdom is proved right by my actions

I will not stop but I will move on, I will produce my fruit

The little pebble that others reject will

one day become a stepping stone

Someone is waiting for me & my ideas

Someone is waiting to say yes

I will say next & I will receive my reward

I Am A Winner

Everyone loves a reward. Everyone wants to WIN. We all want to be rewarded for our deeds. For hard work, we want to be compensated for a job well done. A simple reward when you work is to enjoy life, to be happy. For many people today it is difficult to find stable employment much less a job that provides financial stability lasting through retirement. You want a career from which you can enjoy a comfortable lifestyle, one from which you can pay all your bills and still have left over funds with which you can spend enjoying with family and friends.

Do you borrow money or sell your possessions so that you may eat, pay bills and merely make a living? When you borrow, you become a slave to that from which you borrowed. There is no reward in borrowing. It may seem like the easy way out, but there is no positive benefit when in the long run your lifestyle suffers from the high price one experiences from living in debt. As your living situation begins to deteriorate, reality starts to set in as you realize the full weight of high cost debt keeping you as a slave often times for many years, especially if you are the only one striving to pay off that debt.

Through all your trials and failures you should know that there is a reward coming for all the hard work and all the good that you do. Be not afraid to persevere and continue to go after what you want in life, be strong and you will be rewarded. Some day soon you will be released from your struggles and the difficulties that you face. As you set challenging yet realistic goals and accomplish them, eventually, you will rid yourself of hardship. You will obtain your liberty, joy and happiness.

> *"Infinite striving to be the best is man's duty; it is its own reward. Everything else is in God's hands."*

MAHATMA GANDHI

When you are *truly* rewarded you receive a fair return for your efforts. You are then motivated to maintain and improve your behavior. Meaningful rewards involves more than money or material gain. Sometimes just the little things in life can make you feel rewarded. A simple recognition by name, an engaging conversation or a hug can make you feel appreciated and rewarded. When someone tells you thank you or even gives you a thank you note, you feel rewarded. Fun loving random acts of kindness are always a welcomed reward, they nurture your self-esteem and they make you feel good.

A child wants a reward for being obedient and following his parents' demands. A child looks forward to and responds well to positive reinforcement for good behavior. Psychologists say that behavior is based on motive. If a pleasant response occurs from your behavior, you are more likely to repeat that behavior. A reward is sometimes seen as approval of good behavior. So children might think that if they do something good that their parents will love them more or will reward them for their good behavior. So, like children, adults believe that when they do good things, something good will happen.

"The highest reward for a person's toil is not what they get for it, but what they become by it."

JOHN RUSKIN

When do you get rewarded? When you reward others. When do you get ahead? When you help someone else to get ahead. When do you make your millions? When you help someone else to make their millions. When do you win? When you help someone else to win. Think about a time when you were rewarded, what happened? How did it make you feel? What can you do to reward others? Use this affirmation knowing that you will be rewarded for all that you do.

Start now and write your own **My Reward** affirmation:

>*>*>*>*>*>*>*>*>
_____
_____
_____
_____
_____
_____
_____
_____
_____
_____
_____
_____
_____
_____
_____
_____
_____
_____

AFFIRMATION # 11

Gratitude

On this day, I choose to be grateful

No more excuses, no more stories of sorrow & despair

I am giving them up for a better life & future

I am making a difference; I will get it right this time

I am giving up all my excuses; I will not place blame

I am grateful for the truth

I am grateful for the world around me

I am experiencing real joy

I am educating myself & learning about life

I am grateful for my basic needs that are provided for me

I am grateful for life and all that it has to give

I Am Thankful

Gratitude involves being thankful and expressing gratefulness in spite of any obstacle. Gratitude is further defined as a feeling or an attitude in acknowledgement of a benefit that one has received or will soon be received[3]. The attitude of gratitude is related to positive thinking. Gratitude also involves taking action to expressed thanks. Gratitude is a source of encouragement or a coping response used when situations or events are not going well. When you focus on your gratitude, even though, you feel burdened, rest a sure that nothing unfavorable lasts forever, and situations can be changed for the better. When you are grateful, you choose to express sincere appreciation to another, and in turn you receive pure joy through the experience.

"As we express our gratitude, we must never forget that the highest appreciation is not to utter words, but to live by them."

JOHN F. KENNEDY

Gratitude is an inner choice to feel thankful for a person, a thing, a gift, an experience, a thought, an event, or a situation. When you express gratitude, especially during times of unpleasantness, you soon recognize the underlying opportunities and valuable potential.

---

[3] http://en.wikipedia.org/wiki/Gratitude

Gratitude benefits not only the person who receives it, but also the person who shows it. A sense of gratitude gives you feelings of accomplishment and satisfaction. Being grateful can also be a protection for your health. Appreciating life and having the knowledge of good health, helps you to be more pro active to prevent sickness and disease. Being grateful makes you feel more emotionally and spiritually balanced. When you are emotionally and spiritually in tuned, you handle stress better, you are more relaxed and at peace with yourself.

"Gratitude unlocks the fullness of life. It turns what we have into enough, and more. It turns denial into acceptance, chaos to order, confusion to clarity. It can turn a meal into a feast, a house into a home, a stranger into a friend."

MELODY BEATTIE

Imagine if tragedy or disaster happens in your life. Do you stop being a loving, caring and kind person? Do you begin to feel alone as if you have no one? Would you still feel grateful and hold fast to your integrity or do you become depressed and want to give up? Sometimes disaster happens in our lives and we wonder why. Why is this happening to me? When things cannot get any worst, you fall ill and your body gives out from all the stress. Would you still be grateful if you are sick and no one comes to visit you? Would you feel hopeless and helpless? Depression has caused many individuals to want to give up on life. But even when you are feeling down, try to muster a positive word. Try to see some glimmer of hope; you will soon see that depression lifted.

If you are feeling down on your life, if you feel like you cannot handle any more distress, use this affirmation to be grateful for what you do have in spite of the situation or circumstance. Do not be overwhelmed by life, do not despair; you will be delivered from your troubles because you and those that you love were meant for greatness. Just believe and know that things will work out for the good.

"Develop an attitude of gratitude, and give thanks for everything that happens to you, knowing that every step forward is a step toward achieving something bigger and better than your current situation."

BRIAN TRACY

Daily writing in a journal of what you are grateful for during the day can increase your well-being and outlook on life. Having images or visible reminders of what you are most grateful for helps increase your level of gratitude awareness. Speak gratitude to others and choose to be associated with grateful individuals to let their attitude of gratitude constantly rub off on you.

What are the things that you are most grateful for? Who are you most grateful for? What experiences are you grateful for? Focus on these things on a daily basis.

Start now and write your own **Gratitude** affirmation:

>*>*>*>*>*>*>*>*>

_____

_____

_____

_____

_____

_____

_____

_____

_____

_____

_____

_____

_____

_____

_____

_____

_____

_____

_____

_____

AFFIRMATION # 12

Where I Want To Be

I am where I want to be

I am enjoying my success

I am enjoying my wow moments

I have everything that I want

I am making connections

I am walking in my purpose

I am singing for all to hear & see

I am a super Star

I am a living legacy

I am living in divine glory

I am where I want to be

I Am Where I Want To Be

Where do you want to be right now? What do you see? What do you hear? Are you where you want to be? Are you working the job that you love and want to do? Are you making the money that gives you the liberty to enjoy the things in life that you want to enjoy? Are you in a relationship that helps you to grow as a person? Are you in that spiritual place of peace and wellness? Are you physically fit and in good health? Are you emotionally stable and well in you body, spirit and mind? Are your where you want to be? Everything that you have done so far in life has led you to the place where you are right now. Your thoughts and actions have determined your path so far.

"I have a dream that my four little children will one day live in a nation where they will not be judged by the color of their skin, but by the content of their character."

MARTIN LUTHER KING, JR.

The seeds or ideas that you plant today will germinate into a certain kind of tree. You decide what kind of tree that will be. Take 100% accountability for your life. Do not blame your mother, father, spouse, brother, sister, children or other family for where you are today. Break free from the blame cycle. This will never get you anywhere. You made your ultimate choices. If things did not turn out as you expect it, that is OK, once you have breath in you, you can still try and change things. Life is not for the feeble heart, as a weak heart soon gives out and dies away. Let the passion inside you burn bright. Let your light shine! Listen to that inner voice that tells you that you can be where you want to be right now.

> *"I might not be where I want to be, but thank God I'm not where I used to be. I'm OK, and I'm on my way!"*
>
> PAUL WHITE

> *"You have brains in your head. You have feet in your shoes. You can steer yourself in any direction you choose. You're on your own, and you know what you know. And you are the guy who'll decide where to go."*
>
> DR. SEUSS

Change where you are right now by changing your thinking and start doing things differently. Push past your fears, get the support and help you need to succeed. Start making connections with others, network with those that can get you where you want to go. Get the information that you need to be where you want to be. It feels so good to overcome fear and accomplish a goal. Start enjoying your success now. You never know until you try. Start enjoying your "wow" moments, yes, you did that and you can do so much more. You went there and you can go so much farther.

You have all that you need to be where you want to be. Be the great person that you *truly* are. To be great, you have to fight many battles and win. It may be a struggle, but you have to stay focus and push through with all your might. Sometimes your success comes when it seems like it cannot get any worse. Just when you are on the verge of giving up or letting go, your success comes. Just keep pushing forward, try and try again. Act as if you are already there, even when you do not see it. Once you have accomplished where you want to be. You can then sit back and enjoy your victory!!! Obstacles will come, but know that you can succeed. You can pull through, and be victorious.

"There are a lot of steps between where I am and where I want to be. The real task is- How can I make each step fun?"

UNKNOWN

No time like the present to enjoy your success than now. You are a Super Star. No time like the present to be a living legend. No time like the present to make an impact on those around you. You are where you want to be.

Start now & write your own **Where I Want to Be** affirmation:

>*>*>*>*>*>*>*>*

AFFIRMATION # 13

My Voice

My voice is powerful

My voice is full of majesty

My voice can break hard wood,

My voice can make your heart skip a beat

My voice can soothe your wounded soul

My voice can set your heart on fire

Like a lion in the jungle, my voice can tame the wild

My voice speaks of wonderful & glorious things

My voice gives strength and praise

My voice leads me to discover my passion

My voice rings on forever more

I Am Using My Powerful Voice

You can know a person from the sound of their voice. Everyone's voice is unique and different. A voice can be loud or quiet, high or low, rough or smooth. A certain voice can inspire you or put you into severe depression. A voice can touch you to the core and enlighten your soul. A voice can uplift you or put you down, can make you laugh or make you cry, make you happy or sad. What great power a voice has. It causes a shift in the atmosphere, it moves you or causes you to remain still.

People respond to the sound of a voice. That's why music is so powerful, we respond to a certain song by how it makes us feel. Just from their voice, a certain singer can move you to the core. The most successful singers have voices that enlighten your heart and soul; make you feel loved. Listening to the voice of Teddy Pendergrass, it makes women at his concerts get excited and throw their underwear on stage. His voice is described as a husky baritone, equivalent to the likes of Barry White. Women see men with a deep voice as manly, sexy and attractive. A deep voice is also said to be alluring and captivating.

How majestic it is when you hear a sweet melody that is enchanting and engaging, it could go on and on for days. It makes you happy and full of joy.

How you use your voice is up to you. If you can speak, be grateful. How frustrating it is to want to speak and nothing comes out of your mouth or what you want to say comes out garbled. Try talking to someone who is dumb or who has trouble saying what they want to say because of a stroke or brain injury. What would you do if you lose your voice and you cannot speak again? This is one of the scariest thing for a singer or someone that uses their voice professionally, but even for the lay person. If you do not have a voice, you have to find other ways to express yourself.

"Your time is limited, so don't waste it living someone else's life. Don't be trapped by dogma- which is living with the results of other people's thinking. Don't let the noise of others' opinions drown out your own inner voice. And most important, have the courage to follow your heart and intuition."
STEVE JOBS

You choose how you use you voice. For something to happen, you have to say, "let there be and there will be." You can choose to be positive or negative, encouraging or discouraging. Whatever you say to someone will be heard, whether they choose to respond or not. Begin to understand that your voice has power and whatever you say goes somewhere and something will happen as a result. Look at what is preventing you from using your voice, to be all that you can be. Now look at what specific action steps that you can take to remove obstacles that get in the way of how you express yourself.

"If you hear a voice within you say 'you cannot paint,' then by all means paint, and that voice will be silenced."

VINCENT VAN GOGH

Learn to use your voice wisely, to help to build up and not to tear down and destroy. Start with your self-talk. Think of your inner voice. Take time to pause, relax, breathe, listen and reflect on what you tell yourself. Look back on what you have been telling yourself that has led you to where you are right now.

Questions

Is your inner voice positive or negative? What kind of images, emotions or physical sensations does your inner voice produce? Once you release that inner voice, how are you using your outward voice? What do you say? What do you hear? How does your voice affect your family, friends and other relationships? How does it feel to use your voice to achieve your goals? What can you do to make your voice be known and be more productive? What will it take to make this a reality?

Make a plan of action to use your voice more wisely. You do not want to be someone who is like an empty barrel who speaks all the time and does nothing. Whatever you say has been put out there in the atmosphere. Follow through with the action of your voice. Your voice is action. They say action speaks louder than words, I agree, they do, but the thoughts and words come before the action. Speak words of kindness to yourself daily.

Start now and write your own **My Voice** affirmation:

>*>*>*>*>*>*>*>*>*>*>*>*>*>

_____

_____

_____

_____

_____

_____

_____

_____

_____

_____

_____

_____

_____

_____

_____

_____

_____

AFFIRMATION # 14

I Am Living

Life is worth living

Life is worth loving

I am physically present & showing my visibility

I have an energy and a power source that pushes me on

I am enjoying the joy & experience of going through life

I am dynamic and energized

I have what I need to meet my needs

I am taking action to carry on

I am responding on my own behalf

I do not merely exist, but I am really living

I Am A Living Legend

Each passing year on each birthday, we celebrate life. We celebrate one more year living on this earth, being with family and friends. One more year to make contributions toward a future generation. One more year of opportunity, fulfilling your dreams and your heart's desires. One more year making your mark on this world. One more year loving and supporting someone. One more year living, laughing and enjoying life. One more year achieving your full potential. One more year living your passion. One more year being happy!

"Somebody should tell us, right at the start of our lives, that we are dying. Then we might live life to the limit, every minute of every day. Do it! I say. Whatever you want to do, do it now!" There are only so many tomorrows."
POPE PAUL VI

Without the breath of life, we are just like a lump of clay, just dirt! We then have no use, no real purpose. When we die, our bodies will return to dust and our spirit returns to God that gave it. It is interesting to see people who just go about life casually without fulfilling their goals. They are living dead. They are frozen and caught up in the mundane way of life. They are in a job or relationship that they hate, but they just compromise because they are afraid to change. But this is not natural, that is why our mind, body and soul cry out and tells us that we need to change because if we do not change the situation, the situation will change us.

At times there can be risks in changing a situation, however, developing the courage despite the risks, can lead to a fulfilling life. You will not get time back once it has passed and one day you may lose your opportunity to do or say what you always wanted to do and say. Yesterday is gone; today is another day. Time is not always on our side. Not everyone gets to live to see a hundred years old. Be encouraged to start taking action and start living the life you always wanted. Change your way of thinking and change your way of living.

Questions

Are you really living or are you just going day by day without taking risk and in search of the fruits of your labor? Why do you work so hard and still you are not producing all that you desire? Are you leaving behind a legacy for others to follow? What is your legacy for your children and your children's children? What will they say when you die? When you look upon your life, what do you see? Can you say it was a life worth living and would you do it all the same again? Would you change some things?

"I've always lived a life where people have said, 'Look at him. Who does he think he is?' And who I think I am is someone living life to the brim."

ED VICTOR

Risk being happy, having joy and doing something that enriches your life. What is the worst case scenario? What are you willing to do to be happy? You have what you need to meet your needs and respond on your own behalf. You only have one body; you have only one life to live because there is only one you. This may sound like a cliché, but sometimes fantasy mirrors reality. Your dreams can become a reality.

How come some people get to live out their dreams? Why can't we all do what we love? What makes anyone person better than the other? There is so much living to be done. You can not travel the whole world and see all that is there to see. There are so many adventures in life to enjoy, these far outweigh reasons not to find enjoyment. There is so much to enjoy and there is much not to enjoy, but why choose the latter? Life is short, start living yours today!

Start now and write your own **I Am Living** affirmation:

>*>*>*>*>*>*>*>*>*>*>*>

AFFIRMATION # 15

I Am Loved

Have the strength to withstand any storm

I am worthy to be praised and to be honored

In my distress, I will consider myself loved

I will cry out and be heard

I will not be afraid of those who do not love me

I will fly like an eagle and soar on the wings of love

I am delivered from those who come against me

I am a delighted because I am protected

I am a true treasure; I am loved

I Am Loved

Love conquers all. Love is very powerful. To overcome fear, just show love. There is no fear in love. If you have fear in your love life, your love has not been perfected. What is love? Love is showing patience, honor, compassion, understanding and kindness. Love strengthens and builds up. Love makes you feel content. True love produces a state that brings you joy, peace and satisfaction. We were all born to love. The relationship of a mother and baby can be so loving. The love between a man and woman is the ultimate union of mankind. A loving person is sincere, conscientious, bold, truthful and focuses on what is good for all versus self. A loving person is not envious, boastful, arrogant, resentful, rude or selfish. A loving person is not easily irritated. In loving ourselves, we learn to love others.

Love is a force more formidable than any other.
It is invisible- it cannot be seen or measured; yet it is powerful enough to transform you in a moment, and offer you more joy than any material possession could."
BARBARA DE ANGELIS

There is something about love that is majestic and that is transcending; it moves your very core. That is why love songs, movies, poems and stories are so powerful. Risk loving those who hate you. Risk being a living sacrifice to do what is right in spite of how people treat you with jealous disregard and selfish cruelty.

You say, how can I be loving and giving to someone who is contentious, hateful and despiteful of others. How does a loving person go astray? You have to be loving in spite of but not at the risk of your emotional and physical well-being. You deserve the best that life has to offer. You deserve to be treated with respect, honor and praise. Do not fall short or conform to the negativity of this world. Do not say it is OK to be bad because everyone else is being bad and doing wrong. A loving person hopes, tolerates, believes and endures all things, but not at the risk of losing oneself.

"Being deeply loved by someone gives you strength, while loving someone deeply give you courage."

LAO TZU

Risk speaking love, but also showing that love; otherwise you are not being real. You are just making noise with mere words with no real substance, how deceitful and superficial. Nonetheless, no matter how kind you might seem; if you do not have love in your heart, you are nothing. When you consider yourself loved, you love yourself and you love others. A loving person does not think of self, but of the welfare of others. A loving person lay down their life for the greater good of all. With love, you have the strength to withstand any storm. When you are loved, you feel like you are on top of this world.

"Where there is love there is life."

MAHATMA GANDHI

With I am loved affirmation, start focusing on being a more loving person. You become loving by envisioning the environment you want to create through the power of love. Practice being a more loving you. Exercise your heart muscle to be more physically and mentally fit. Some scientific studies suggest that a fun and loving relationship can bring health benefits such as reduced stress, lower blood pressure and a longer life. Be specific about what a more loving you looks like, feels like and sounds like.

Questions

What are the activities that you enjoy that evoke a more loving you? What is one specific circumstance that you can remember that you felt very loved? Ask yourself how would a more loving you affect your family and other relationships? What does a more loving you look and sound like?

Think of the things that have prevented you from being a more loving person. Think about what skills and other resources you currently have, or able to develop, that can aid in your ability to be more loving. Focus on those specific action steps you can take to be more loving today. Whether in a long or short span of time, it benefits no one to be unkind. The love you share will magnetically attract positive outcomes in your life.

Start now and write your own **I Am Loved** affirmation:

AFFIRMATION # 16

My Comforter

I am my comforter

I may feel lonely, but I am never alone

My comforter resides inside of me

My comforter gives me guidance and protection

My comforter speaks within my heart and tells me where I should follow

My comforter is witty and smart

My comforter is loving and kind

My comforter gives me peace and happiness

My comforter fills me up till I overflow with joy

My comforter is all knowing, tells me what to say and do

My comforter is forever present

I Am Comforted

A comforter is one who comforts. From the time of conception and you were in your mother's womb you had a comforter. Maybe that is why babies cry when they are born as they are missing that comfort they felt when they were in the womb. Imagine having someone from birth and throughout life that is your guide and is there watching over you, telling you what to do and where to go. You have a helper that guides you to accomplish your priorities (large or small). Who is your helper? Who is this guide that helps you to get things done? In times of brokenness, grief and despair, there is an inner voice that speaks to you and steers you in the right direction.

A comforter keeps you grounded, keeps you safe and protects you from the bitter elements of life. Sometimes you wonder how you are able to do and have the knowledge about certain things. There is an inner, invisible force within you that keeps you aligned; that keeps you grounded. That same force prompts you to make decisions between right and wrong; to make solid decisions on whether to say yes or no. This inner guide acts as your internal radar, it foretells danger when something bad is going to happen, and helps you to navigate a clear path to avoid danger.

Some believe that intuition is an inner guide that gives you the ability to know certain things without the use of reason or logic. Intuition has been seen as that inner guide or comforter that helps you in times of need. We are more than a mere intuitive past. Your Spirit helps you to realize you are the most powerful creation in existence upon the planet. As part of the creation process, you were given dominion to rule over this earth. Not to be proud, self-righteous, arrogant, conceited, over-confident, swollen with pride, but to be loving, kind, humble, peaceful, and intelligent enough to do what's right for the benefit all.

> *"O that our hearts were enlarged in love to God,*
> *that we might turn inward, to the blessed comforter,*
> *that the blessed Jesus said the Father would send."*
> **ELIAS HICKS**

Sometimes you may forget that God innately gave you a comforter that is within you. You have more than you need within you to help carry you through life. You must take time to realize and connect with one of the most central and empowering thought, that is, you have the ability and the power to overcome any challenge. Learn to stay tuned into you inner guide and comforter that you were born with and that was created just for you. Take time to pause from the often hectic pace of life to relax, breathe, listen, reflect and get in tuned with your inner guide and comforter. Remember that you are wonderfully made, and you have a comforter that will lead you in the path that you should follow. Trust and obey your comforter because of this added source to life, you have access to powerful living.

Remember a time when you felt truly comforted. How did that

make you feel? What does your vision of a more comfortable life look like? What can you do now to create more comfort in your life?

That innate part of our being has help us to go through situations and survive. Some behaviors depend on certain things to happen in our lives for us to really get an understanding of who we truly are. We all want to be comfortable and take control.

Start now and write your own **My Comforter** affirmation:

>*>*>*>*>*>*>*>*>

AFFIRMATION # 17

My Mind

I am changed through the renewal of my mind

My mind is transformed into new thinking

My mind is now focused on learning

For wisdom is what I seek

I am committed and will not give up

I am thinking, acting and growing in good judgment

I am gaining knowledge & understanding

My mind is open and helps me to grow

My mind gives me the strength to carry on

I will love with all my heart, all my soul and all my mind

I Am Renewing My Mind

Your mind includes your imagination and thoughts. The mind is defined as element of a person that enables them to be aware of the world and their experiences; to think, reason, perceive and feel. The mind is a product of the brain. The brain is the physical manifestation of the mind. The mind is not tangible. The mind is not located anywhere in physical space even though we view and talk about the mind and the brain as the same. You have a mind that carries out specific functions, to stimulate you to behave in a certain manner.

> *"If my mind can conceive it, and my heart can believe it, I know I can achieve it."*
> **JESSIE JACKSON**

The mental power that you possess allows you to differentiate between right and wrong. You have a mind that allows you to take full control against adverse situations that could be a detriment to your well-being. You have a mind to stand up for your rights. The thoughts that you have can be programmed by your circle of influence. Some adults hold on to those things that was told to them when they were children. A parent in mindless anger and rage may tell a child that they are lazy and will not amount to anything. That child may in turn, call herself or himself "Lazy Susie or Lazy Johnny" for the rest of their lives because their mother or father called them that name. They may be the most productive person, but instead they resort to the name. As adults, they may also end up calling their own children "Lazy Suzie and Lazy Johnny", leading to a generation of individuals believing that this stigma is a family heritage.

Individuals can get caught up in their own convictions, calling it the truth, because everyone says so. Let no one deceive you with words having hypnotic appeal, or so called "words of wisdom" fashioned according to the tradition of man. Nonetheless, there are those who are sincere, well meaning and do give good advice and guidance. You have free will. You have to decide against lofty, baseless opinions or ideas raised as the truth. Get the facts. You have to read between the lines. Let no one mentally deceive you and captivate you with their words. They may say that this is what everyone is saying or this is what everyone is doing. But you have to decide against worldly opinions raised as the truth. Think twice. Think twice again. Use your mind to see what is not fully seen. Use your mind to seek wisdom and understanding. Be in a constant stage of renewing your mind and seeking knowledge.

The mind is documented as having the capability of producing around 70,000 thoughts daily; meaning that a new thought is generated every 1.2 seconds/86,400 seconds per day.[4] Obviously with the many things that go through your mind, you have the power to change your way of living by changing your way of thinking. You can really change who you are by changing your thoughts. Your goal then if you're not satisfied with the present course in which your decisions are taking you, is to immediately engage in a thought renewal and a transformation process.

---

[4] http://wiki.answers.com

> *"All wrong-doing arises because of mind. If mind is transformed, can wrong doing remain?"*
>
> BUDDHA

Every minute, every second, there are many things that go through your mind. How can you change your way of living by changing your way of thinking? Can you really change who you are by changing the way you think? How do you renew you mind? If things are not going right in your life, how can you to start thinking and doing things differently?

Some key things to do in order to begin your mind renewal process as you ponder how you can you start thinking and doing things differently.

Gather good knowledge and seek wise understanding that will stretch you to learn and think positively. Take correction to learn new ways of thinking and get involved in diverse activities. Really take a second look at what is happening in your life. Start to examine and formulate forecasts for your life in the future weeks, months and years from the moment you begin to make changes. Do not accept or settle for negative, deficient, impoverished, depressing and unhealthy ways of being. Do not conform and believe that you have to be and do like everyone else.

> *"Put your heart, mind, and soul into even your smallest acts. This is the secret of success."*
>
> SWAMI SIVANANDA

Deep down in your subconscious mind you know what you

have to do. Start to change the things that are not working for you. Be quick to listen and be slow to speak. Let all bitterness, anger, harsh words and slander be put away from your mouth. Anger can mentally block you from really being open to the kind of life that you truly seek. Do not be shaken to wrath or wrong doing. Do not get so angry that you do not act and think right. Be humble, slow to anger and you will have much more understanding.

How do you have a mind that is content and filled with peace? You cannot control how someone else acts or behaves, but you can take control of your thoughts, feelings and actions. You have self-control. Be open and be clear-minded. Do not be influence by things that give you the sense of feeling great when in actuality you are destroying your mind and your body. Do not let any substance control you. Individuals who over indulge in drugs and alcohol to feel better are being deceived and are on a down ward path to destruction. Too much of anything is never good; sometimes a small interaction of the wrong kind of drug can lead to death and utter destruction. Look ahead towards the goal of upward thinking. Use your positive mind affirmation to get you on the right path. Mentally persevere. Press forward to have mental peace, good wisdom and understanding.

Start now and write your own **My Mind** affirmation:

>*>*>*>*>*>*>*>*>*>*>*>

AFFIRMATION # 18

My Peace

I will not worry about anything

I will not worry about how I will be fed or what I will wear

Worrying is not helpful, it takes away my time

Worrying does not add value to my life

I know what I need to do and I do it

I seek peace and chastise any stumbling block

I will choose what is best and it will not

be taken away from me

I will set my heart on receiving what was meant to be

I will focus on claiming God's will for my life

I will have peace and be at rest

I Am Enjoying My Peace

What is stopping you from making peace with someone? Why is it so hard to reconcile? Why is it so hard sometimes for people to agree with one another? People say they want peace but they would rather watch a major title fight than be involved in a event for world peace. Millions of dollars are spent each year in the "sport" of fighting than in missionary causes for peace. Children see their parents fight and emulate this behavior. Children today grow up with more violence on TV, in music, in games, and on the internet. Mahatma Gandhi is one of the most influential person in the 20th century who stood up for peace. One man made a difference by using love, incredible faith and courage to overcome violence. Wouldn't it be wonderful if this was a world where everyone lived together in peace? We need to promote and encourage peaceful activities and behavior. The peace in this world depends on us all! The popular 'We are the world' song says "It's true we'll make a better day, just you and me."

"When the power of love overcomes the love of power the world will know peace."
JIMI HENDRIX

When you humble yourself, it is easier to have peace with yourself and with others. Be encouraged to speak peace at all times. Break down the walls of hostility. It may be difficult to not want to fight back against someone who has done you wrong, but because you love yourself, you will be peaceful. In so doing you will put negative people to shame. When you are not at peace it affects how you think and behave. It is a good thing to have a peaceful mind. A peaceful mind gives you clarity. Where there is peace, there is love and happiness. When you have peace, you do not feel afraid. Peace brings inner contentment and security. When you have peace you able to have good rest or sleep well at night. Peaceful people live longer and have more enriching lives. Your desire in life should be about living a life filled with peace.

We all have different lives growing up. There are times in life when you were picked on, abused or bullied. How does an individual whose family was slaughtered still remain at peace? They say bad people relate to violence and brutality and that is the only way to respond to these kind of people. When someone does you wrong, are you going to give then a piece of your mind or are you going to have peace in your mind?

> *"An eye for an eye only ends up making the whole world blind."*
> **MAHATMA GANDHI**

Where there is anxiety, mistrust, stress, worry, fear and frustration there is no peace. If there is no peace there is conflict. Conflict is the source of many wars and crimes being committed. When families are not at peace with each other they are more likely to cause civil disruptions and domestic disputes. When there is disturbance of the mind and body, there is no peace. This uneasiness sometimes causes disease, pain and suffering. When there is constant upheaval, the body is not at rest. You are constantly fighting instead of producing calm and tranquility. The lack of the body's ability to produce physical stability increases the production of chemicals that causes harm or dis-ease (free from ease). Stress and anxiety causes changes in the bio-chemicals of the body that can affect your health and cause physical illness. When we are at not peace, our subconscious mind responds to the body and releases hormones that cause pain, increased blood pressure, palpitations, muscle tightness and even death.

Can you be 100% stress free and at peace, no matter the circumstances? Why do we worry so much, even though the time spend worrying does not really help the situation. There will be times that you will encounter stress, but it is how you deal with that stress that makes the difference. There is an inner strength and power that comes from being humble, tolerant and patient, regardless of the situation. Your thinking is much better when you are not swayed or easily overcome by heightened negativity. How can you have peace undisturbed by negative people and circumstances? Forgiveness is a big part of being peaceful. If you are able to forgive someone for the wrong that they have committed against you, it benefits you more than the other person by bringing you peace that you cannot understand.

"Every goal, every action, every thought, every feeling one experiences, whether it be consciously or unconsciously known, is an attempt to increase one's level of peace of mind."

SYDNEY MADWED

Meditation, visualization and positive affirmations are great ways that you can use to create peace in your life. Through meditation, visualization and positive affirmations, comes added success. The world's most super successful individuals have used meditation to help them fulfill goals and create ideas that enrich their lives. Meditation has helped individuals to deal with emotional issues and relationship difficulties. Meditation gives you an inner strength and self confidence to overcome conflict and stressful situations to see the world as a better place.

In order for your affirmations to be effective you have to meditate on them day and night. Meditation is a great tool used to distress and create mental peace. It helps you to contact, restore and strengthen your connection to your deepest self, to that subconscious mind that is part of your inner core. Meditation gives you mental clarity to focus on those things that you need to focus on the most. It allows you to focus on your strengths; it promotes psychological and spiritual well-being, and maturity. It gives you the capacity to be fully present to what is happening within and around you. You learn to be more fully present in the moment and not be drawn into distractions and reactions.

"This life that has been given to us as a gift, as such a precious gift. To really try to understand it, really try to recognize it, is the greatest meditation. Through the media of this knowledge we can tap into our inner sources that are so beautiful."
PREM RAWAT

Meditation enables you to respond rather than react. Meditation allows for the flow of your greatest ideas; it allows what is deep inside and your essential truth within to emerge. It allows for authentic change to occur. It allows you to listen to that inner voice of wisdom. When you first start the practice of meditation, just be open to the experience and what it is has to offer. With practice, meditation can strengthen and support a growing clarity, peace, calmness and serenity to your life. The important approach for this practice is just to take notice and redirect your thoughts without judgment or evaluation. For centuries and in countries all over the world, this is a simple practice with extraordinary outcomes for prosperity in every area of your life.

You may say that you want peace, but do you really know what that peace looks like. With visualization, you see yourself has already accomplishing your goals. To have peace in your life, visualize yourself as already living a peaceful life. Visualize what that peace would look like. We have a photographic memory, so our minds are stimulated by pictures and things that we can see. To enhance your visual world of peacefulness, gather pictures, images and sounds that evoke peacefulness. Create and keep an environment of peace, so that peace will follow you. Who would you want to be with? Be around people who bring peace into your life. Write about activities that would create more peace in your life. Think about a time when you felt very peaceful and think about what you would have to do to attain that peace all the time.

Start now and write your own **My Peace** affirmation:

>>*>*>*>*>*>*>*>*>*>*>*>

AFFIRMATION #19

My Victory

I will be careful of those that flatter with their tongue

But their insides are filled with wickedness

There is no faithfulness in their mouth

I know that they will fall by their own wrong doing

I know that whatever they do will not last forever

It is only for a time that will soon pass away

I will encourage those that are trust

worthy, loving & supportive

I will stand up for what is right

I have protection that covers me as a shield

I will win the battle & I will have my victory

I Am Victorious

You have remained steadfast in many trials, so no matter what you are going through right now, you can still stand the test of time. Do not be tempted to do wrong. Choose to remain victorious when you are encouraged to do something wrong, continue to stand up and not be drawn into temptation by your own selfish pleasure. In order to have the victory, you have to be strong. You must do all that you can do to stand firm in your convictions. Interestingly, during times of temptations and major challenges, incredible and valuable lessons leading to strengthen your future can be learned.

"If you believe in yourself and have dedication and pride - and never quit, you'll be a winner. The price of victory is high but so are the rewards."

PAUL BRYANT

Through difficulty, it is a time to learn and demonstrate how strong and mighty you are. It is during times of difficulty that you learn about how much more accomplished you are positioned to become. Be teachable and open to new ideas. A problem may seem so huge or greater than you can fix, but just have hope that everything will work out for the good. You can have success or triumph over battle, struggle or some difficulty, regardless of situations. You are victorious when you are pursuing your goals, standing firm and fulfilling your purpose.

Victory is the act of defeating an enemy or opponent in battle or other competition. Life can seem like a constant battle or struggle against difficulties or obstacles. You have to endeavor against all odds to overcome and be successful in spite of the odds. You get your victory when you set out to achieve a goal and you are able to successfully achieve it in spite of all that you face. You get your victory when you set out to achieve a goal and you are able to successfully achieve it. You get the victory because you stand strong although you might not have received the response or results to a certain situation. You were made to overcome every difficulty you face in spite of the circumstances. You were created to be victorious!

"Far better is it to dare mighty things, to win glorious triumphs, even though checkered by failure... than to rank with those poor spirits who neither enjoy nor suffer much, because they live in a gray twilight that knows not victory nor defeat."

THEODORE ROOSEVELT

Sometimes you have to see your victory in the little things that take place each day. Big victories are often times accomplished with the completion of many small ones. Just simply driving or going out each day and surviving to return home is a victory. Not everyone returns home after leaving to come back. The ability to breathe fresh air is a victory. You have the victory because you are able to see the wonderful world around you and enjoy nature, listen to the birds' singing, see the bees buzzing around, see the beauty of flowers and wondrous trees. You have the victory because you can hear and communicate when someone speaks to you. You have the victory when you can just listen. You have the victory when you are loving and receptive to others. You have the victory when you can walk or run two miles when you thought you could not even take a step at all. You have the victory because you can move your body when others are too weak to even squint their eyes. You have the victory because you understand your definition of yourself, you have no need to adopt a false identity in order to become like someone else; you fearlessly represent who you are.

Think of a time when you experience a victory. What would you have to do to create more victories in your life? Write your victory affirmation. Visualize what your new victory looks like. How do you want to feel? What do you need to do to make it happen?

Start now and write your own **My Victory** affirmation:

>>*>>*>*>*>*>*>*>*>*

AFFIRMATION # 20

I Have The Power

I was born with the power that gives me strength

I have a mighty mind, body and soul that carry me on

I will use my power to do great things

I will use my power to build, restore and lift up

I will use my power to be creative and do good work

I have the power to act on my behalf and

to help those who are in need

I have the power to overcome negative

things, people and situations

I have the power and authority to overcome my fears

And nothing by any means will hurt me

I have the power to say peace, be still

I have the power to make a difference in the world

I Am Powerful

The most powerful people in the world usually include heads of states, CEOs, kings and even religious leaders. These individuals are said to have access to certain amount of human and economic resources. They have influence on worldly events. Everyone of us has the potential to influence our environment. You have the strength to do all things that you set your mind to do. Your brain would not work if it was not for the power of the electrical signals and connections being transmitted through your body right now. In order to even think you need energy (power). The cells in your body need energy to become activated. At the heart of every cell is a nucleus. A nucleus contains mitochondria which are known as "cellular power plants". When there is a situation, you have the power to respond, fight or flight because the cells in your body are busy working hard to protect you from harm. The power within you is the key to your survival.

> "Nearly all men can stand adversity, but if you want to test a man's character, give him power."
> ABRAHAM LINCOLN

> "Character is power."
> BOOKER T. WASHINGTON

Negativity drains the power that is within you. Have you ever wondered sometimes, why you feel so weak when you are in certain situations. Negativity from your surroundings and others around you transmit negative energy towards you. Notice the next time that you go somewhere and due the negativity, you start to feel weak and weighed down. You are pushing against negative elements real and imagined.

Deep within your body, the cells that are not actively sending messages are slightly, negatively charged. Since everything relies on the power signals inside of you, anything negative causes a breakdown in your body's power system. This causes a depletion of your inner resource. You have been drained! But, your ultimate power source and life decisions belong to you. You have the power to direct your life. You have the choice to live in the positive. You have the power to repel negative energy, people and situations. Let your power source shine. There is something great, energizing, illuminating and supernatural when you see someone who is using his or her power (energy in positive deeds) for the greater good. It gives you strength and it makes you want to shine.

Most leaders are powerful because they are able to exercise a lot of influence over others. Individuals with power have access to vital resources. But, man only has so much power. Man cannot control all the elements of this world. Man's influence can only go so far. Out supreme source is God. He can give us all that we ask for.

> *"The most common way people give up their power*
> *is by thinking they don't have any."*
> ALICE WALKER

Start now and utilize the power that you have inside of you. Understand that you have the ability and strength to control your life. Forgive and forget past regrets and disappointments that have come into your life, learn from them. Stop engaging in reflective thoughts of what you did not do, cannot do, should not do and have not done. Stop feeling guilty for the past. The past is the past. Let go of any and all past mistakes. Learn from the past. It will take time and some work to focus on the positive and the power source within you. We have been conditioned and rooted to focus on the negative, but if you want all that you were meant to have, you have the power to get just that.

Do not give your power away. When you are lazy, you give your power away. When you procrastinate, you give your power away. When you avoid, you give your power away. When you do not control your negative and harmful impulses, you give your power away. Refuse to indulge in unnecessary and useless behaviors. Overcome and resist the urge to choose the "easy way" out. Discipline yourself to reject immediate satisfaction, pleasure or comfort. Choose to control your behavior or response instead of being ruled by it.

Use your time, energy and strength wisely. Use your mental power to your advantage. When you make a decision, follow through with perseverance until it is accomplished. Instead of thinking and focusing on the worst case scenarios that can happen, always concentrate on the best possible scenarios.

Put your focus and attention on the positive and enhancing things in life that make you feel good. Spend time each day gathering knowledge and reading inspirational or informative books. With knowledge comes power. Get the power words to build yourself up. Get the understanding to figure out how to tap into your power source. Make physical and spiritual happiness your number one priority. We were all born with and given the power and authority to do certain things, to make an impact on this world. When you use your power (energy) for good, you will increase well being and remove stress and disease in your life. Find ways each day to use your power to do something good for someone else.

Use your power to take time out to enjoy the simple things in life. When was the last time that you had a good belly laugh? Laughter has long-term health benefits, improving your mind, body and spirit. When was the last time you had fun while you worked? When was the last time you had fun with family and friends? When was the last time you went for a walk in the park with family or friends? When was the last time you went off the beaten path and did something adventurous? How are using your power? What are you using your energy and strength to do?

No time like the present to start using your power to build yourself and start doing what you love. You have the power to change people's life, including your own first. When you work the power that is inside of you will do exceedingly above all that you thought you could do. Start now to find out how you can be a more powerful person. Start to make changes for the better. With will power you can bring out the inner strength inside of you which is vital to your success in life. To be a powerful person, you have to take action.

Start now and write your own **Powerful** affirmation:

>*>*>*>*>*>*>*>*>

AFFIRMATION # 21

I Am Fulfilled

I hear and have understanding

I see and have awareness

My ears are open to hearing

My eyes are open to seeing

My mouth is filled with praise

I will receive all the goodness that comes my way

I am determined to push through and follow on

I am well able to stay in my purpose

My vision will be fulfilled

I Am Being Fulfilled

In all that we do and where we go, we will return unto one place. In the journey of progressing and moving forward in life, it is very important to know that it is not all about riches, as riches come and go. Since you came into this world with nothing, so you will have nothing when you die. Even though the *golden* King Tut wanted to be buried with all his treasures, his riches are not with him today. King Tut riches are in a museum, used as historical display and points to ponder in social conversations.

Now that you have read this book, you have started to focus on what brings you true happiness, joy and fulfillment. While you were growing up you may have been led to believe that there were certain things you were supposed to accomplish, and once you did accomplish them, you would feel fulfilled. These mental stimulants are at work inside of you, driving your belief in a natural way that one day you will be successful as these "things" come together.

> *"The intelligent man is one who successfully fulfilled many accomplishments, and is yet willing to learn more."*
>
> ED PARKER

Fulfillment is the process whereby something is made complete. You feel fulfilled, when you have reached your goals and when you have achieved certain levels of accomplishments that you have set for yourself. Wouldn't you like to set out to do something (execute) and go out (performance) and get it (fulfillment)? The more you talk about your goals to the right people and how you want to accomplish them, it creates an inner drive or desire that eventually affect further development. Who are the right people? First pray to God about your goals. Subsequently, speak to a life coach or a friend who can give you tangible feedback, resources and the support that you need to make your goals a reality.

In satisfying your needs, you have to focus on the journey that at times things may seem difficult, but you must be willing to choose and explore action steps that are available. Look at the early explorers who believed that the earth was not flat and that they would not fall off the edge. These explorers first believed in themselves and they were determined to achieve their dreams. They went through much opposition from others, fearful at times of even making an attempt of trying to accomplish anything at all.

These explorers were ridiculed and became at odds with the prevailing ideologies of the time. They lacked finance, but they were able to bring back gold and many treasures from distant lands. They stepped out to endure months of sailing and laboring on rough oceans, but they took on the challenges to accomplish what they seek. They were self-directed and self-motivated. They took on the tasks at hand and persisted in spite of the odds.

Through self-determination and motivation, Neil Armstrong became the first known person to walk on the moon. Alexander Graham Bell was able beat out his competition to be known as the inventor of the telephone. It is said that his competitor's **failure to**

take action led to Bell's favor in gaining his great recognition[5]. The Wright brothers conquered powered flight with the first airplane, *The Wright Flyer or Flyer 1*. In their test runs for flight, they tried and tried many times until they succeeded and they were eventually able to maintain flight for a certain time period. They had personal and professional obstacles. These two brothers did not even have a high school diploma[6], but they did not let that stop them from gaining knowledge, starting their own businesses, and following their dreams to produce one of the world's greatest invention. It is because of their trials and errors that we are able to fly in a plane today and travel the world in a few hours without being bound at sea for days and days.

Despite his hearing impairment, Thomas Edison was one of the most prolific inventors in history. He was able to bring the invention of the light bulb and many more devices (battery for electric car, mechanical vote recorder, recorded music, etc.) to the American main stream[7]. According to Edison, you should be "brave and courageous!". When you are following your dreams you will go through trials and errors. Whatever the setbacks you encounter, you can come back stronger and be more prosperous. You just have to have faith and keep working on all those ideas that you have in your head. But, without works, that faith is dead.

---

[5] Wikipedia. Elisha Gray and Alexander Bell telephone controversy.

[6] Wikipedia. Wright Brothers.

[7] Wikipedia. Thomas Edison

In the process of getting our needs fulfilled, you want to use positive affirmations to help reduce the tension and stress that comes from a lack of fulfillment of needs.

"I believe each of us has a mission in life, and that one cannot truly be living their most fulfilled life until they recognize this mission and dedicate their life to pursuing it."[8]

BLAKE MYCOSKIE

Imagine what invention and ideas you have lying dormant inside of you. Imagine what dreams and vision you have bubbling up inside. You could have a cure for diseases or an invention that could make life so much more simpler. Focus on the passion to fulfill your goals and desires. With passion there is excitement, there is energy and there is vigor. If you do not like your current outcomes, you have to start to change you current thoughts and responses. Assume that the world is the perfect place right now. Start to design what it should look like.

Consider the early explorers and inventors who are ordinary individuals, but they believed in themselves, they thought outside the box and they achieved extra ordinary success. For things to make an impact, you have to think outside of this world, you have to think BIG. Go outside and look up, there is a huge world out there. Imagine the great places and great inventions that you can discover. Imagine how many people you can affect, just by fulfilling your dreams. Change

---

[8] All quotes are from www.brainyquote.com

your self talk with affirmations and with positive affirmations, life changing ideas will flow into your mind.

What does it mean to you to be fulfilled? What would it take for you to be fulfilled? When are you going to start fulfilling your dreams and work on your passion? When are you going to start fulfilling your Spirit? Focus on those things that make your life more fulfilling. Gather the knowledge and take action steps everyday towards a more fulfilling life.

Start now and write your own **Fulfilled** affirmation:

>*>*>*>*>*>*>*>

Epilogue

Thank you for reading this book. I hope that you were inspired and touched by the words that you have read as I have been in writing them. No time is better than now to start writing your own personal life affirmations. Through affirmations, you can begin to have a more meaningful experience with life. Start to focus more on what you can do right now. Develop a attitude for life planning. Be a *go-getter* and not just a *thinker*. Start taking action; otherwise you are denying yourself from the powerful life that you say you want to live.

Once you have written down your affirmations, you have searched within and you have written down your goals as already been accomplished. Liberate yourself. Go straight away and start working your way to success.

There is no time like the present to start enjoying life. Use affirmations to become more focused and start fulfilling your inner potential. Please let me know if you need help and if you have any comments or questions that you would like to share. I would love to hear from you.

For purchasing this book you can use the provided discount code in your email subject header to get help in completing your own personalize life-skills affirmation script. Through affirmations, the possibilities are endless in creating powerful living!!!

Group discounts available. Get copies of this book for your family, friends, business, church or organization.

Email: Lifeskillsdevelopment@yahoo.com

Affirmation discount code: Lifeskillsaffirm

Affirm Yourself and Your Organization: The Life Skills Affirmations Workshop

>*>*>*>*>*>*>*>

Positive and powerful changes occur when individuals, businesses, organizations, and churches experience *The Life Skills Affirmations* Workshop. You will be inspired and motivated to make changes and turn your life around. *The Life Skills Affirmations* Workshop will empower you to be more productive with less effort; this will help you to be a more effective person in your everyday experiences. Training and motivational seminars can also be designed for your organization or company & individual needs. *The Life Skills Affirmations* Workshop is ideal for groups such as:

- Churches
- Nonprofit organizations
- Small businesses
- New retirees, students and new hires
- Women's group

With affirmations, you can express your unique abilities so that the world will see you and want to gravitate towards you. You can then say "yes" to the *good*, say "no" to the *bad*, so that you will have room in your life to say "yes" to your greatness.

For more information:

E-mail:Hmcfar1022@aol.com

Twitter- Lifeskillscoach@skillscoachtwit

Book Recommendations

(Support Local Authors)

Bullies, Buddies & Bangers, Dr. Michael Bell

Constant Contact, Dr. Michael Bell

Cascade, Marjorie Dunkley (Available on www.Xlibris.com)

Everlasting Benefits Of Obedience, Michael Jones (Available on www.Amazon.com)

Revive The Champion In Me: No Weapon Formed Against You Will Prosper, Michael Jones

The Kingdom of Tickledom, Marjorie Dunkley (Available on www.Amazon.com and www.Xlibris.com)

Additional Resources

Support Local Missions/Churches (*Ask not what your church or ministry can do for you, but ask what you can do for your church or ministry*).

Christ Global Church. 6800 Sunset Strip, Sunrise, FL 33313. www.christglobalchurch.org. Founder, Pastor Michael Jones on a mission to support the spiritual needs of individuals locally and internationally demonstrating Jesus' love for all people. Feeding over 300 poor homeless individuals in Fort Lauderdale, Florida, building homes for individuals in the Philippines, taking care of children in Haiti, Jamaica and Pakistan. Worship time on Saturdays begins @10:30am. Email: Theglobalchurch@yahoo.com Tel: 1-877-764-7235 or 954-298-9479.

Heaven Bound Deliverance Church of God. Following God's commandment to love one another as he has loved us. 1490 South Military Trail, Suite 4, West Palm Beach, FL 33415. Pastor Hector Peart. Tel: 561-531-6396. Worship time on Sundays: 11:00am. Sunday School: 10:00am. Special Prayer on Mondays at 7:00pm. The Best Bible Study: Wednesdays @7:00pm. Fasting on Thursdays at 10:30am-12:30pm.

Harvest Treasure Foundation. Saving lives with good nutrition. Teach children them how to eat healthy by planting fruit and vegetable gardens in schools. Teaching children how to plant, reap and eat their own harvest, encouraging them to teach others at home and make this healthy habit available again for children and families around the world. Put prayer back in schools, say "Yes", sign petition online. Founder, Sylvia Palomino: 561-856-5289.

www.harvesttreasure.org.

Seacrest Seventh Day Adventist Church. A place of healing and restoration. Involved in education and community outreach. www.seacrestsda.org. 101 NE 12th Ave, Boynton Beach, FL 33435. Senior Pastor, Frederick Maragh. Email:seacrestsda@gmail.com. Tel:561-536-5539. Saturday Worship Service @ 11:00am. Community Outreach @ 3:00pm.

Second Opportunity Ministries II, Inc. is a ministry dedicated to reaching out to children around the world who needs someone to show them the love of Jesus Christ. This Ministry provides an environment where children are safe, eat three meals a day, and receive an education and vocational training through programs designed to meet their emotional, physical and spiritual needs. Send your support to Evangelist Yolanda Blandford:561-541-0762, Mailing Address: PO Box 22127, West Palm Beach, Florida 33416. Email:Yolanda.blandford@gmail.com. Get more information at www.secondopportunitiesministries.org

Sonshine Family Worship Center is a ministry dedicated to Christ and sharing the love of God with the World. Worshiping at the Kevin Harvin Center, 1030 Royal Palm Beach Blvd., 2nd floor, Royal Palm Beach, Florida, 33411. Senior Pastor & Founder, Ronald J. Mcfarlane. Mailing Address: PO Box 212163, Royal Palm Beach, Florida, 33421. Tel/fax:561-340-2131.

St John CDC, INC: A Non profit organization that provides health and social service related services for children, adults and senior citizens, make available office space for health care practitioners, and support positive social activities for the youth and young adults. 119 E Pender St, Wilson, NC 27893. www.stjohncdcwilson.org. Exec. Director: Rev. Dr. Michael S. Bell. Email:mbell81353@aol.com. Tel:252-265-9764.

www.ingramcontent.com/pod-product-compliance
Lightning Source LLC
Chambersburg PA
CBHW040220240426
43662CB00030BA/15